MILITARY CAREERS

JOBS IN THE NAVY

by Sloane Hughes

BEARPORT
PUBLISHING

Minneapolis, Minnesota

Credits

Cover, © Pacific Press Media Production Corp./Alamy Stock Photo and © Petty Officer 2nd Class Leon Vonguyen/DVIDS; 5, © Petty Officer 2nd Class Kelsey Eades/DVIDS; 6–7, © Washington Navy Yard / Wikimedia Commons; 9, © Chief Petty Officer Diana Quinlan/DVIDS; 10–11, © Darwin Lam/DVIDS; 12–13, © Seaman Matthew Dickerson/DVIDS; 15T, © Senior Airman Rebeckah Valladares/DVIDS; 15B, © Stacy Laseter/DVIDS; 17, © Petty Officer 2nd Class Michael Lindsey/DVIDS; 19T, © Petty Officer 2nd Class Juel Foster/DVIDS; 19B, © Petty Officer 3rd Class Ryan Mayes/DVIDS; 21T, © Courtesy Photo/DVIDS; 21B, © Petty Officer 3rd Class Brandon Roberson/DVIDS; 22–23, © Petty Officer 2nd Class Arthur Rosen/DVIDS; 25T, © Russ Stewart/DVIDS; 25B, © Petty Officer 1st Class Byron Linder/DVIDS; 27T, © Leonard Weston/DVIDS; 27B, © Petty Officer 2nd Class Daniel James Lanari/DVIDS; 28T, © Mass Communication Specialist 3rd Class Dylan Lavin/DVIDS; 28B, © Mate 2nd Class Damon J. Moritz/Wikimedia Commons; 29, © United States Navy SEALs/Wikimedia Commons, © Gary Nichols/U.S. Navy/Wikimedia Commons, and © Petty Officer 2nd Class Jason Isaacs/DVIDS.

Bearport Publishing Company Product Development Team

President: Jen Jenson; Director of Product Development: Spencer Brinker; Managing Editor: Allison Juda; Associate Editor: Naomi Reich; Associate Editor: Tiana Tran; Art Director: Colin O'Dea; Designer: Kim Jones; Designer: Kayla Eggert; Product Development Assistant: Owen Hamlin

Statement on Usage of Generative Artificial Intelligence

Bearport Publishing remains committed to publishing high-quality nonfiction books. Therefore, we restrict the use of generative AI to ensure accuracy of all text and visual components pertaining to a book's subject. See BearportPublishing.com for details.

Library of Congress Cataloging-in-Publication Data

Names: Hughes, Sloane, author.
Title: Jobs in the Navy / by Sloane Hughes.
Description: Minneapolis, Minnesota : Bearport Publishing Company, [2025] |
  Series: Military careers | Includes bibliographical references and
  index.
Identifiers: LCCN 2024012512 (print) | LCCN 2024012513 (ebook) | ISBN
  9798892320405 (hardcover) | ISBN 9798892321730 (ebook)
Subjects: LCSH: United States. Navy--Vocational guidance--Juvenile
  literature. | United States. Navy--Juvenile literature.
Classification: LCC VB259 .H84 2025 (print) | LCC VB259 (ebook) | DDC
  359.002373--dc23/eng/20211209
LC record available at https://lccn.loc.gov/2024012512
LC ebook record available at https://lccn.loc.gov/2024012513

Copyright © 2025 Bearport Publishing Company. All rights reserved. No part of this publication may be reproduced in whole or in part, stored in any retrieval system, or transmitted in any form or by any means, electronic, mechanical, photocopying, recording, or otherwise, without written permission from the publisher. Bearport Publishing is a division of Chrysalis Education Group.

For more information, write to Bearport Publishing, 5357 Penn Avenue South, Minneapolis, MN 55419.

CONTENTS

Offering Aid 4

History of the Navy .6

Joining the Navy .8

Combat Careers 12

Eyes in the Skies 14

Building and Fixing 16

Information Gatherers 20

All Hands on Deck. 24

Many Jobs for Sailors 26

More about the Navy .28

Glossary. 30

Read More. 31

Learn More Online. 31

Index. 32

About the Author 32

OFFERING AID

Aboard a swaying U.S. Navy hospital ship, microbiologists peer at glass dishes under **microscopes**. They are taking a close look at an **infectious** disease that is making people sick. These scientists are working hard to stop the disease from spreading. By studying illnesses, navy microbiologists help develop new vaccines that keep people all over the world healthy.

Sailors in the United States Navy have many important jobs that help the nation. Microbiologists are just some of these seamen!

CAREER SPOTLIGHT: Microbiologist

Job Requirements:
- 17 to 41 years old
- 5 weeks officer training
- Officer

Skills and Training:
- Laboratory Operations
- Research & Analysis
- Advice & Consultation

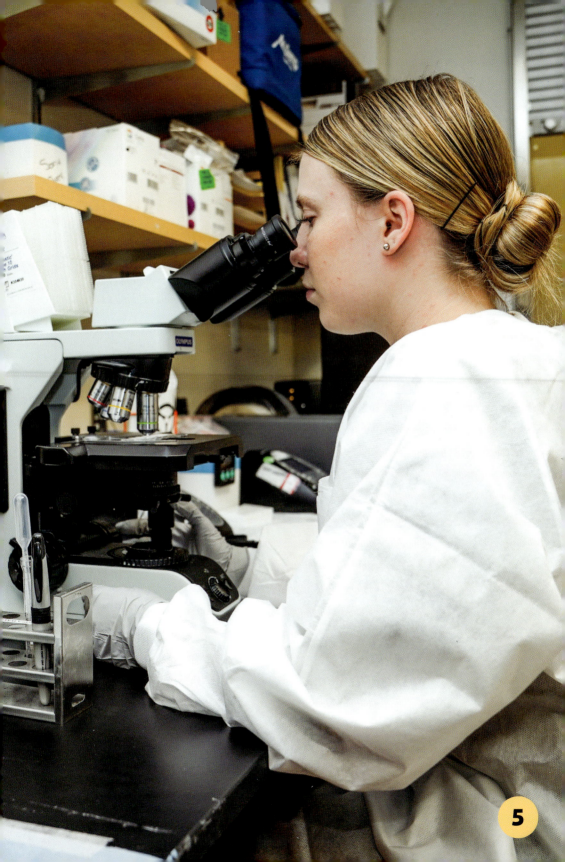

HISTORY OF THE NAVY

The United States Navy was first formed during the Revolutionary War (1775–1783). Its job was to protect the waters around the colonies and prevent supply routes from being attacked by British ships. After the country won its freedom, the navy was broken up. However, threats at sea remained, both from pirates and other countries.

At first, the U.S. Navy had only two official ships. Today, it has more than 280 **vessels** ready to be sent around the globe.

In 1794, the navy was formed again to protect the waters and people of the young United States. Today, the U.S. Navy is not just a fighting force. It also sends ships to help with disaster relief and to rescue **refugees** or others lost at sea.

A navy ship attacking a British vessel during the Revolutionary War

JOINING THE NAVY

For **enlisted** sailors, the first step to joining the navy is a career test. Based on personality, skills, and interests, the test results show the jobs best suited for each navy **recruit**.

Next, the recruits enter boot camp for 10 weeks. They learn basic navy skills, such as tying the many knots needed on boats. Recruits practice firefighting skills, train with weapons, and learn first aid. They also run drills to learn how to face **combat** challenges that may lie ahead, such as what to do if the ship is under enemy attack.

During boot camp, recruits must also pass a test that includes swimming 50 yards (46 m) and floating facedown in the water for 5 minutes.

Different tests help recruits prepare for challenges on the job.

Near the end of boot camp, recruits must complete an exercise called Battle Stations. For 12 hours, future sailors go through several **simulated** challenges based on actual events. They take turns keeping a lookout on deck while having little or no sleep. They practice rescuing shipmates and how to respond to a flood. The recruits also put out practice fires and repair broken ship parts.

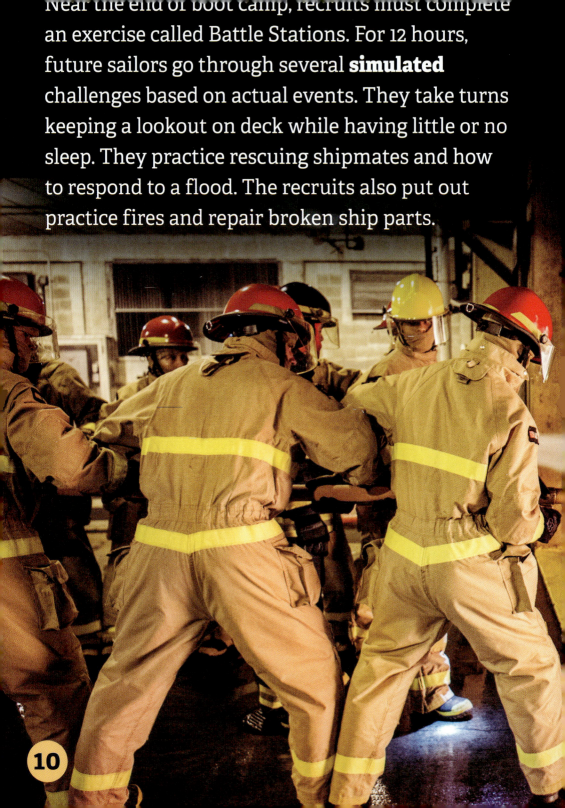

After completing Battle Stations, recruits graduate basic training. They officially become sailors in the U.S. Navy.

★ ★ ★ ★ ★ ★ ★

Most members of the navy are enlisted sailors. They report to officers who get special training to lead others on **missions**.

COMBAT CAREERS

After training is complete, some sailors' jobs take them to combat zones. A gunner's mate makes sure all weapons on board a ship are ready for each mission. They check for damages and make repairs as needed. Then, these sailors prepare and test the weapons to be sure they are in working order.

For secret missions, the navy sends Sea, Air, and Land (SEAL) teams. These **special operations** teams are able to slip into and out of enemy territory without notice. SEALs may collect information on enemy plans or capture terrorists. SEALs also destroy enemy beach obstacles for troops to safely come ashore.

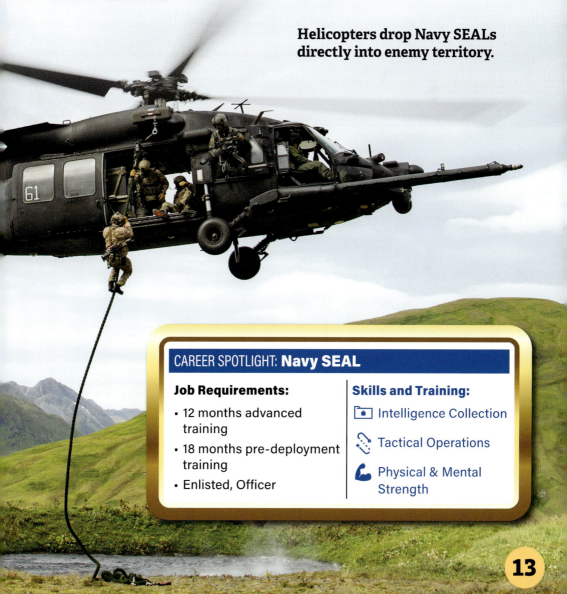

Helicopters drop Navy SEALs directly into enemy territory.

CAREER SPOTLIGHT: Navy SEAL

Job Requirements:
- 12 months advanced training
- 18 months pre-deployment training
- Enlisted, Officer

Skills and Training:
- Intelligence Collection
- Tactical Operations
- Physical & Mental Strength

EYES IN THE SKIES

Air teams are the navy's eyes and ears in the sky. Fighter pilots collect **aerial** photos and videos to find enemy locations. They may also attack enemy aircraft and help defend the ground and sea forces below.

Along with fighter pilots, naval aircrewman avionics search for enemy submarines or other underwater threats. They detect and analyze information using both **sonar** and aerial photos. Then, these sailors pass along the information to navy sea teams to help during battle.

CAREER SPOTLIGHT: Naval Aircrewman Avionics

Job Requirements:
- 19 weeks technical training
- 2 to 18 weeks aircraft training
- Enlisted

Skills and Training:
- Sonar Operations
-  Communication Systems
-  Intelligence Reporting

Fighter pilots flying an aircraft

15

BUILDING AND FIXING

The Navy's Construction Battalion, also known as the Seabees, are builders. Seabee divers work in underwater construction teams, clearing **wreckage** and repairing damaged ships. They are also trained to defend themselves in case of enemy attack.

Some Seabees **specialize** in steelwork on land. They build permanent military bases and temporary camps around the world. Navy steelworkers also help with disaster relief, fixing broken roads and rebuilding destroyed homes.

CAREER SPOTLIGHT: Navy Steelworker

Job Requirements:
- High school diploma
- 11 weeks advanced training
- Enlisted

Skills and Training:
- Maintenance & Repairs
- Construction & Engineering
- Hand & Power Tools

16

Navy steelworkers getting their hands dirty while working on a construction job

Sometimes, there are broken pipes or damage to the outside of a ship. Hull maintenance technicians create replacement parts out of many materials, such as aluminum, steel, copper, brass, or iron. Machinist's mates monitor **nuclear** aircraft carriers and submarines. They usually work in nuclear reactor rooms, where this energy is being made. These sailors ensure that fleets have enough power at sea.

CAREER SPOTLIGHT: Hull Maintenance Technician

Job Requirements:

- 13 weeks engineer training
- 5 weeks technical training
- Enlisted

Skills and Training:

- Maintenance & Repairs
- Problem-solving
- Organization & Planning

Hull maintenance technicians wear face shields to protect their eyes as they work.

INFORMATION GATHERERS

Since the U.S. Navy often works at sea, changes in the weather and water affect how sailors do their jobs. Meteorology and oceanography officers monitor the weather and ocean conditions, keeping a lookout for incoming storms or difficult currents. They map out the safest paths for ships to take.

Weather is only one part of nature that sailors encounter. Entomologists are sailors who study insects that may carry diseases. They identify bugs and where they came from. This helps entomologists develop **pesticides** to keep ships free of insects.

CAREER SPOTLIGHT: Entomologist

Job Requirements:
- 18 to 41 years old
- 5 weeks officer training
- Officer

Skills and Training:
- Identification & Strategy
-  Data & Information
-  Biological Studies

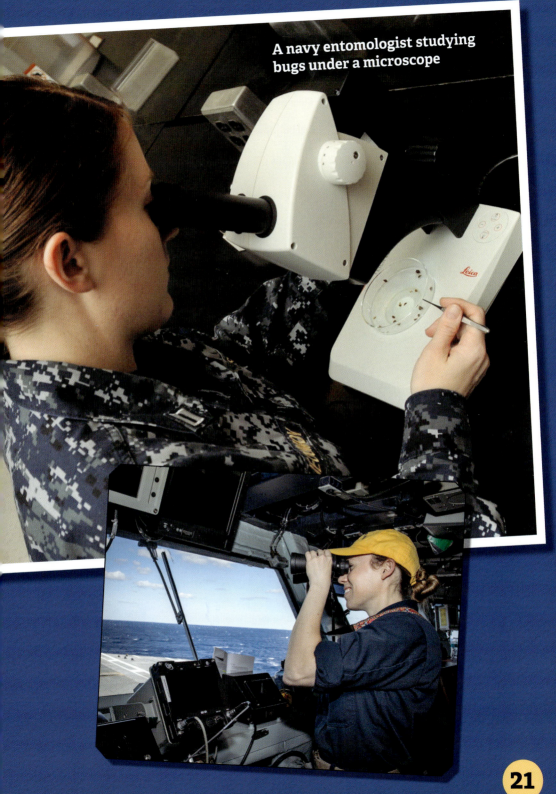

A navy entomologist studying bugs under a microscope

Some navy jobs require collecting and analyzing information to help plan and complete missions. Quartermasters read maps and charts to navigate the open oceans. They tell pilots where to go.

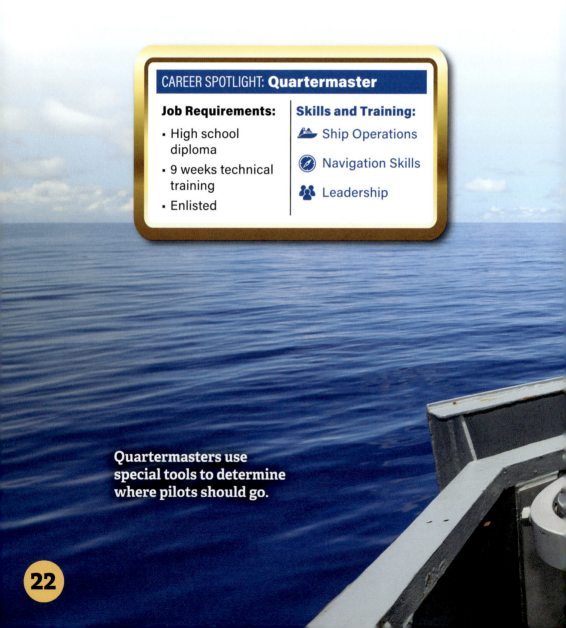

CAREER SPOTLIGHT: Quartermaster

Job Requirements:
- High school diploma
- 9 weeks technical training
- Enlisted

Skills and Training:
- Ship Operations
- Navigation Skills
- Leadership

Quartermasters use special tools to determine where pilots should go.

Cyber warfare engineers work with information in a different way. They research, develop, and test the best **software** and **firmware** to protect computer networks from being taken over or shut down by the enemy. These engineers also target enemy computer systems to gain important information.

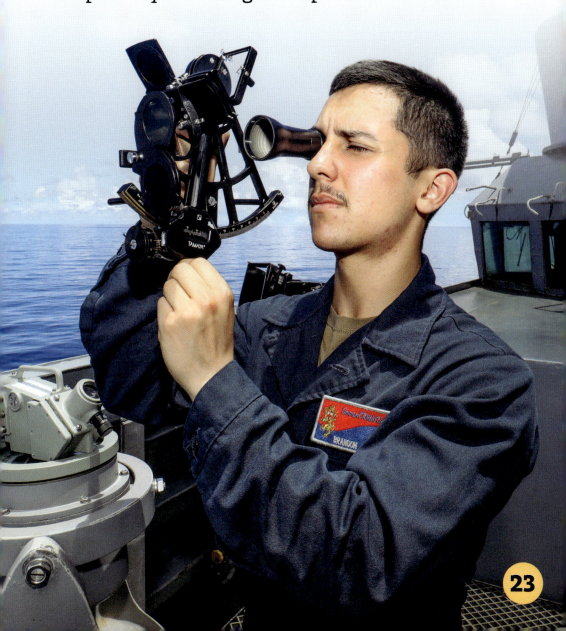

ALL HANDS ON DECK

Life on a vessel is like a community. Navy culinary specialists plan healthy and balanced meals around the clock for hungry sailors. Sometimes, they even cook special meals for foreign **dignitaries** visiting the ship!

Sailors need great hearing in the navy. An audiologist regularly gives hearing tests to be sure sailors are aware of sounds around them. These specialists also teach sailors to protect their ears from loud noises by properly putting in earplugs or using other ear protection.

CAREER SPOTLIGHT: Audiologist

Job Requirements:
- 18 to 41 years old
- 5 weeks advanced training
- Officer

Skills and Training:

 Health & Wellness

Health & Safety Operations

 Audiology

25

MANY JOBS FOR SAILORS

Some navy jobs are a lot like those in civilian life. Navy chaplains lead religious services for sailors, including weddings and funerals. Damage controlmen respond to fires and rescue people from danger. The navy band holds workshops and recitals to teach youth in the community how to play many styles of music.

Whether stationed on bases or ships, the sailors of the U.S. Navy have many important jobs. Together, they work hard to protect the country and its people.

CAREER SPOTLIGHT: Damage Controlman

Job Requirements:	Skills and Training:
• High school diploma	Firefighting
• 10 weeks technical training	Welding
• Enlisted	Carpentry

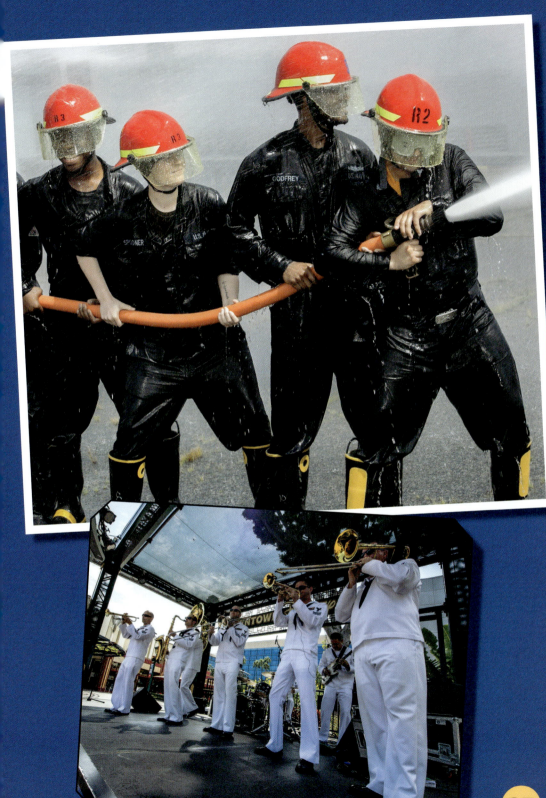

MORE ABOUT THE NAVY

AT A GLANCE
Founded: October 13, 1775
Membership: More than 400,000
Categories of ranks: Enlisted sailor, warrant officer, and commissioned officer
Largest base: Naval Station Norfolk in Virginia

DID YOU KNOW?

★ Most experts say the United States has the strongest navy in the world.

★ Large navy ships called aircraft carriers are often named after presidents, such as the USS *Abraham Lincoln* and USS *George Washington*.

★ Bill the Goat has been the U.S. Naval Academy mascot since the early 1900s.

Bill the Goat

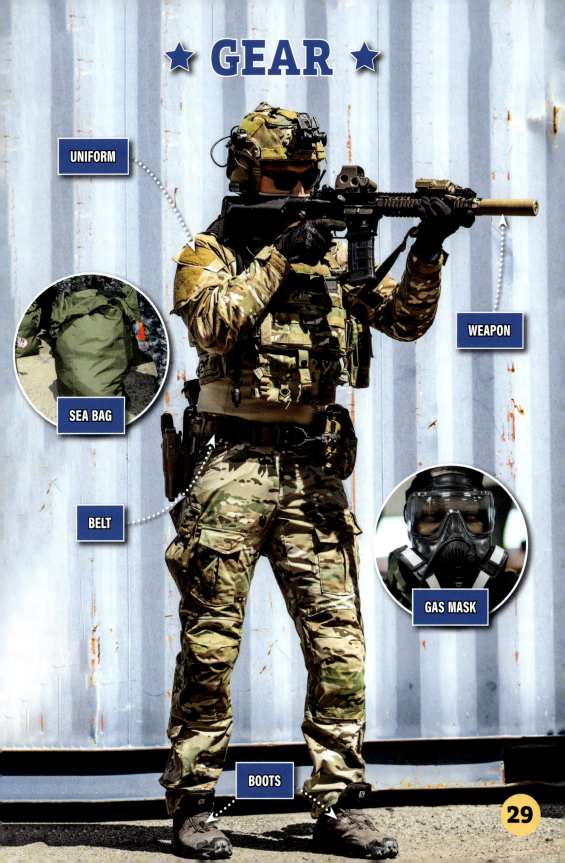

GLOSSARY

aerial of, relating to, or occurring in the air or atmosphere

combat fighting or having to do with fighting between people or armies

dignitaries people of high position or honor

enlisted soldiers who have joined a branch of the armed forces without prior special training and hold a rank below officer

firmware computer programs contained in a hardware device

infectious spreading or capable of spreading rapidly to others

microscopes instruments consisting of a lens for magnifying images of small objects

missions tasks that have a particular goal

nuclear having to do with a type of energy that is produced by splitting atoms

pesticides substances used to kill unwanted insects

recruit a person who is going through the process of joining the military

refugees people who flee for safety, especially to a foreign country

simulated made to look or feel real

software the programs used by a computer

sonar a device for detecting the presence and location of submerged objects by sound waves

specialize to focus on one subject or area of work

special operations a branch of the United States Navy made up of sailors specially trained in intense, on-the-ground warfare

vessels large boats

wreckage the broken and disordered remains of a wreck

READ MORE

Eason, Sarah. *Navy SEALs: The Capture of Bin Laden! (Mission: Special Ops).* Minneapolis: Bearport Publishing Company, 2021.

Ndikumana, Eric. *Jobs in the U.S. Navy (Exploring Military Careers).* New York: Rosen Publishing, 2023.

Phillips, Howard. *Inside the Navy SEALs (U.S. Special Ops Forces).* New York: PowerKids Press, 2022.

LEARN MORE ONLINE

1. Go to **www.factsurfer.com** or scan the QR code below.
2. Enter "**Navy Jobs**" into the search box.
3. Click on the cover of this book to see a list of websites.

INDEX

audiologist 24

Battle Stations 10–11

boot camp 8, 10

chaplains 26

culinary specialists 24

cyber warfare
   engineers 23

damage controlmen 26

entomologist 20–21

fighter pilots 14–15

gunner's mate 12

hull maintenance
   technician 18–19

machinist's mate 18

meteorology &
   oceanography
   officer 20

microbiologists 4

navy band 26

navy SEALs 13

quartermaster 22–23

refugees 7

Revolutionary War 6–7

Seabees 16

ABOUT THE AUTHOR

Sloane Hughes has written numerous books for young readers. She lives on the Great Lakes and enjoys learning about sailing vessels.